A Year to Rer
For Those Whose
19:

*Celebrating your year
1933
A memorable year for*

Content

Introduction: A Glimpse into 1933..5

Chapter 1: Politics and Leading Events around the World
1.1 The Global Stage in 1933: Where Were You?...6
1.2 Leaders and Statesmen: Movers and Shakers of '33..................................11
Activity: Historical Crossword - Test Your Knowledge of '33.............17

Chapter 2: The Iconic Movies, TV Shows, and Awards
2.1 Memorable Films of '33...19
2.2 Prestigious Film Awards and Honors...22
Activity: Movie and TV Show Trivia Quiz - How Well Do You Know '33 Entertainment?..24

Chapter 3: Music: Top Songs, Albums, and Awards
3.1 Chart-Toppers and Musical Trends..27
3.2 Renowned Musicians and Bands of '33..30
Activity: Music Lyrics Challenge - Guess the Song Lyrics from '33..34

Chapter 4: Sports in 1933: A Journey Through the World of Athletics
4.1 Athletic Achievements and Memorable Victories..............................35
4.2 American Sports: Champions and Championship Moments.......40
Activity: Sports Trivia - Test Your Knowledge of 1933 Sports History...43

Chapter 5: Pop Culture, Fashion, and Popular Leisure Activities
5.1 Fashion Flashback: What the World Wore in '33..................................46
5.2 Entertainment and Hobbies...50
5.3 Slang of '33 - The language of the Era..54

Activity: Fashion Design Coloring Page - Create Your '33-Inspired Outfit...56

Chapter 6: Technological Advancements and Popular Cars
6.1 Innovations That Shaped the Future...60
6.2 The Automobiles of '33...65
Activity: Cars 1933 - Wordsearch...71

Chapter 7: Stats and the Cost of Things
The Price Tag: Cost of Living in 1933..74
Activity: 1933 Shopping List Challenge..78

Chapter 8: The Famous Wedding of 1933
The Famous Wedding of 1933..81
Activity: Famous Wedding Triava - 1993 Edition............................89

Special gift for readers..94
Activity answers..95

Introduction

A Year to Remember - 1933
For Those Whose Hearts Belong to 1933

To our cherished readers who hold a special connection to the year 1933, whether it's because you were born in this remarkable year, celebrated a milestone, or hold dear memories from that time, this book is a tribute to you and your unique connection to an unforgettable era.

In the pages that follow, we invite you to embark on a captivating journey back to 1933, a year of profound historical significance. For those with a personal connection to this year, it holds a treasure trove of memories, stories, and experiences that shaped the world and touched your lives.

Throughout this book, we've woven together the tapestry of 1933, providing historical insights, personal stories, and interactive activities that allow you to relive and celebrate the significance of this special year.

As you turn the pages and immerse yourself in the events and culture of 1933, we hope you'll find moments of nostalgia, inspiration, and the opportunity to rekindle cherished memories of th s extraordinary year.

This book is dedicated to you, our readers, who share a unique bond with 1933. May it bring you joy, enlightenment, and a deeper connection to the rich tapestry of history that weaves through your lives.

With warm regards,
Edward Lab

Chapter 1: Politics and Leading Events around the World

1.1 The Global Stage in 1933: Where Were You?

In 1933, the world stood at a crossroads. The Great Depression had its grip on the United States, causing widespread unemployment and hardship. The Dust Bowl ravaged the Midwest, while Prohibition came to an end. On the global stage, leaders like Franklin D. Roosevelt and Adolf Hitler were emerging. Join us as we revisit the pivotal events and prominent figures that defined this year of transformation.

The Great Depression in the United States

In the depths of the Great Depression, the United States faced economic turmoil. Unemployment rates reached their highest level during the winter of 1932/1933, with nearly one in three people jobless. This crisis was a central focus of Franklin D. Roosevelt's incoming administration.

Dust Bowl

The heartland of America, particularly the Midwest, was hit by the Dust Bowl. Strong winds stripped away the topsoil from drought-affected farms, creating devastating Dust Bowls. This environmental catastrophe added to the economic woes of the Great Depression.

Repeal of Prohibition

In a significant shift, the United States repealed Prohibition. The 21st Amendment was passed, effectively ending the 18th Amendment's ban on alcohol. This move allowed for the legal sale of 3.2% beer and wine, marking the end of a notable era in American history.

National Labor Board

The United States government established the National Labor Board (NLB) in August. As part of the National Industrial Recovery Act and National Recovery Administration, the NLB aimed to mediate labor disputes between unions and employers. It consisted of seven members, including labor union and industry leaders, with US Senator Robert F. Wagner serving as chairman. The NLB had limited authority, and President Roosevelt issued executive orders to strengthen it. In 1934, it was dissolved and replaced by the more effective National Labor Relations Board.

CWA Created

To address the unemployment crisis, the Civil Works Administration (CWA) was established as part of the New Deal. It created temporary construction jobs to provide relief to people affected by the economic downturn. The CWA was a precursor to several New Deal programs that aimed to boost employment and stimulate the economy.

Cuba Civil War

In Cuba, a civil war erupted, forcing American businesses to close their operations in the country. This conflict had implications for American foreign policy and its relationship with Cuba.

First Solo Around the World Flight

Aviator Wiley Post achieved a remarkable feat by becoming the first person to complete a solo flight around the world in July. Departing from Floyd Bennett Field in New York, Post made several stops during his journey, including Berlin, the Soviet Union, Alaska, and Canada. He accomplished this feat in 7 days, 18 hours, and 49 minutes, flying a Lockheed 5C Vega named "Winnie Mae." This achievement added to his reputation as an aviation pioneer.

Century of Progress World's Fair

The 1933 World's Fair opened on May 27 and was held in Chicago. It was formally known as the "Century of Progress International Exposition." The exposition was held at Northerly Island near the Museum Campus area of Chicago's lake front. The theme of many exhibits and structures at the World's Fair featured the Art Deco and Art Moderne design styles which were at the height of their popularity and the exposition was intended to provide hope for a better future during the Great Depression. Much of the funding for the fair was provided privately as there was a lack of public resources available. It was set to end in November of 1933 but was so popular that it was extended through October 31, 1934.

Loch Ness Monster

On May 2, 1933, the Loch Ness Monster was sighted for the first time in modern times. This mysterious and legendary creature lurking in the depths of Loch Ness captured the imagination of people worldwide.

1.2 Leaders and Statesmen: Movers and Shakers of '33
Franklin D. Roosevelt

Franklin D. Roosevelt's leadership in 1933 was defined by the New Deal, a transformative set of policies. These included the Civil Works Administration, providing jobs, and the Tennessee Valley Authority, which brought electricity and economic development. His reassuring "fireside chats" instilled hope during the Great Depression, setting the stage for recovery and strengthening the federal government's role in addressing crises.

Adolf Hitler

Adolf Hitler's rise to power in 1933 marked the beginning of a dark and tumultuous period in world history. As Chancellor of Germany, he swiftly consolidated his authority and embarked on a radical transformation of German society and politics. Hitler's contribution, if it can be called that, was the introduction of totalitarian rule in Germany. His leadership led to the suppression of political opposition, the undermining of democratic institutions, and the implementation of repressive policies that targeted minority groups, particularly Jewish citizens. Hitler's actions in 1933 laid the groundwork for the expansion of Nazi power, which would ultimately result in World War II and the Holocaust.

Ramsay MacDonald

Ramsay MacDonald's leadership as the Prime Minister of the United Kingdom in 1933 was characterized by his response to the economic challenges posed by the Great Depression. He sought to address the severe economic crisis through a series of measures aimed at providing relief to those affected. MacDonald's government introduced public works programs and unemployment benefits to mitigate the impact of widespread unemployment. His contribution lay in the efforts to navigate the UK through a turbulent economic period and provide support to the British people during difficult times.

Joseph Stalin

Joseph Stalin's contribution in 1933 was centered on his role as the leader of the Soviet Union. Under his leadership, the Soviet Union continued its ambitious programs of industrialization and collectivization. These policies aimed to transform the agrarian society into an industrial powerhouse. However, they also resulted in widespread suffering and hardship, particularly among the peasantry. Stalin's consolidation of power during this time was marked by a brutal crackdown on perceived political enemies through the Great Purge. While his leadership accelerated the Soviet Union's industrial development, it came at a significant human cost.

Makoto Saito

As the Prime Minister of Japan in 1933, Makoto Saito played a role in guiding Japan through a period of political and social changes. Japan was grappling with the global economic downturn and the challenges posed by a changing international landscape. Saito's leadership was marked by diplomatic efforts, including the withdrawal from the League of Nations, which signaled Japan's increasing militarization and expansionist policies in Asia. His contribution lay in navigating Japan through a complex period of domestic and international transformation.

Joseph Lyons

Joseph Lyons' leadership as the Prime Minister of Australia in 1933 was focused on addressing the economic challenges posed by the Great Depression. His government implemented policies aimed at economic recovery and stability. Lyons' contribution to Australia was evident in his efforts to provide support to those affected by unemployment and economic hardship. His leadership was instrumental in maintaining social and political stability during a period of global economic turmoil.

Activity: Historical Crossword Test Your Knowledge of '33

Are you ready to challenge your knowledge of the significant events and key figures of 1933? Here's a crossword puzzle that will test your understanding of the historic year.

ACROSS

2. This environmental catastrophe in the U.S. added to the economic woes of the Great Depression.
5. The Prime Minister of Japan who oversaw the country's withdrawal from the League of Nations.
6. This U.S. President's New Deal aimed to address the Great Depression.
7. The leader who consolidated his authority as Chancellor of Germany in 1933.

DOWN

1. The Soviet leader who continued policies of industrialization and collectivization.

3. The sighting of this mysterious creature in Loch Ness captured worldwide attention in 1933.

4. The Prime Minister of the United Kingdom who responded to the economic challenges of the Great Depression.

Chapter 2: The Iconic Movies, TV Shows, and Awards

2.1 Memorable Films of '33

In the realm of entertainment, the year 1933 was marked by an array of iconic films that left a lasting impact on the world of cinema. Let's delve into the cinematic highlights of '33:

King Kong

"King Kong," directed by Merian C. Cooper and Ernest B. Schoedsack, stands as one of the most iconic films of the year. This groundbreaking adventure movie introduced audiences to the colossal, stop-motion-animated gorilla, King Kong, who famously climbs the Empire State Building in a thrilling climax. The film's blend of groundbreaking special effects and a compelling story captured the imagination of viewers and solidified King Kong as a cinematic legend.

Little Women

Directed by George Cukor, "Little Women" brought Louisa May Alcott's classic novel to the silver screen. The film's heartwarming portrayal of the March sisters and their coming-of-age adventures resonated with audiences. The cast, including Katharine Hepburn and Joan Bennett, delivered powerful performances, making "Little Women" a beloved classic.

42nd Street

"42nd Street," directed by Lloyd Bacon, was a dazzling and influential musical film that epitomized the spirit of the Broadway stage. Known for its spectacular dance numbers and catchy tunes, the film provided audiences with a glamorous glimpse into the world of showbiz.

The Invisible Man

Adapted from H.G. Wells' novel, "The Invisible Man" was a science fiction-horror film directed by James Whale. The story of a scientist who becomes invisible, only to descend into madness, delivered a suspenseful and eerie atmosphere, showcasing innovative visual effects for the time.

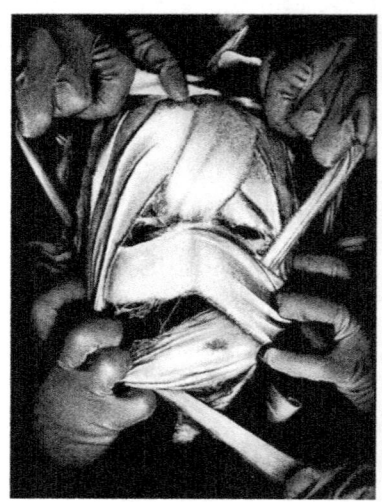

Gold Diggers

"Gold Diggers" was a musical comedy directed by Mervyn LeRoy. Known for its memorable musical sequences and witty humor, the film entertained audiences with its portrayal of aspiring performers and their quest for success.

Duck Soup

Directed by Leo McCarey, "Duck Soup" is a classic Marx Brothers comedy that blended satire, humor, and absurdity. The film is celebrated for its sharp wit and anarchic humor, as well as the Marx Brothers' brilliant comedic performances.

Cavalcade

"Cavalcade" is a 1933 film directed by Frank Lloyd, based on Noël Coward's play of the same name. It won the Academy Award for Best Picture that year. The movie follows the Marryot and Bridges families, showcasing their experiences during significant historical events like the sinking of the Titanic, World War I, and the interwar period. The film's episodic structure offers a historical and personal perspective on British society's transformation. "Cavalcade" is known for its ambitious storytelling and historical scope and remains a notable work in cinematic history.

2.2 Prestigious Film Awards and Honors

The 5th Academy Awards, which took place in 1933, recognized outstanding achievements in filmmaking for the films released in 1932. Here are some of the award categories and their respective winners:

1. Best Picture: "Grand Hotel"
2. Best Director: Frank Borzage for "Bad Girl"
3. Best Actor: Wallace Beery for "The Champ"
4. Best Actress: Helen Hayes for "The Sin of Madelon Claudet"
5. Best Original Story: Frances Marion for "The Champ"
6. Best Adaptation: Edwin J. Burke for "Bad Girl"
7. Best Art Direction: Cedric Gibbons for "The Champ"

8. Best Cinematography: Lee Garmes for "Shanghai Express"
9. Best Short Subject (Cartoon): Walt Disney for "Flowers and Trees"
10. Best Short Subject (Comedy): Hal Roach for "The Music Box"
11. Best Short Subject (Novelty): Mack Sennett for "Speak Easily"
12. Best Sound Recording: Paramount Studio Sound Department for "The Champ"
13. Best Film Editing: Conrad A. Nervig for "Shanghai Express"
14. Best Original Score: Max Steiner for "The Informer"
15. Best Dance Direction: "The Continental" from "The Gay Divorcee"
16. Best Assistant Director: Charles Barton for "Shanghai Express"

Activity:
Movie and TV Show Trivia Quiz
How Well Do You Know '33 Entertainment?

Introduction: Let's test your knowledge of the iconic films and prestigious awards from the world of entertainment in 1933. Choose the correct answers (a, b, c, or d) for each question.

1. Which film featured the colossal, stop-motion-animated gorilla, King Kong, climbing the Empire State Building?
a) Gold Diggers
b) Little Women
c) King Kong
d) 42nd Street

2. Who directed the film adaptation of Louisa May Alcott's classic novel "Little Women" in 1933?
a) George Cukor
b) Merian C. Cooper
c) James Whale
d) Lloyd Bacon

3. "42nd Street" is known for its spectacular dance numbers and catchy tunes, offering a glimpse into the world of showbiz. Who directed this dazzling musical film?
a) Mervyn LeRoy
b) Frank Lloyd
c) Leo McCarey
d) Ernest B. Schoedsack

4."The Invisible Man" is a science fiction-horror film adapted from H.G. Wells' novel. Who directed this suspenseful and eerie movie?

a) Leo McCarey

b) Mervyn LeRoy

c) James Whale

d) Lloyd Bacon

5."Duck Soup" is a classic Marx Brothers comedy celebrated for its sharp wit and anarchic humor. Who directed this satirical masterpiece?

a) Lloyd Bacon

b) Mervyn LeRoy

c) Leo McCarey

d) Frank Lloyd

6."Cavalcade," a 1933 film, won the Academy Award for Best Picture. It follows the Marryot and Bridges families during significant historical events. Who directed this ambitious work?

a) George Cukor

b) Frank Lloyd

c) Merian C. Cooper

d) Frank Borzage

7.What film received the Academy Award for Best Picture in 1933?

a) Duck Soup

b) King Kong

c) Grand Hotel

d) Little Women

8.Who won the Academy Award for Best Actor in 1933 for his role in "The Champ"?
a) Frank Borzage
b) Wallace Beery
c) Leo McCarey
d) Max Steiner

9.The Academy Award for Best Actress in 1933 was awarded to Helen Hayes for her performance in which film?
a) The Informer
b) Little Women
c) The Sin of Madelon Claudet
d) King Kong

10.Which film received the Academy Award for Best Original Story in 1933?
a) The Sin of Madelon Claudet
b) Shanghai Express
c) Bad Girl
d) The Champ

Let's see how well you know the world of entertainment in 1933!

Chapter 3: Music: Top Songs, Albums, and Awards

3.1 Chart-Toppers and Musical Trends

1. Chart-Toppers
The year 1933 witnessed a collection of memorable tunes that resonated with audiences across the nation. Here are some of the chart-topping hits of the year:

"Stormy Weather" by Ethel Waters:
Ethel Waters' soulful rendition of "Stormy Weather" captured the hearts of listeners, making it a standout hit of the year.

"Sophisticated Lady" by Duke Ellington:
Duke Ellington's jazz masterpiece, "Sophisticated Lady," showcased his talent for crafting intricate melodies that continue to enchant music enthusiasts.

"Gold Digger's Song" by Dick Powell:

Dick Powell's rendition of the "Gold Digger's Song" added a touch of charisma to the musical landscape of 1933.

"Lover" by Paul Whiteman:

Paul Whiteman's "Lover" became a musical gem, enchanting audiences with its melodic charm.

"Easter Parade" by Irving Berlin:

Irving Berlin's "Easter Parade" provided a delightful and uplifting melody that became a favorite during the festive season.

"The Last Round-Up" by Billy Hill:

Billy Hill's "The Last Round-Up" brought a Western flair to the music charts, leaving an indelible mark on the year's musical offerings.

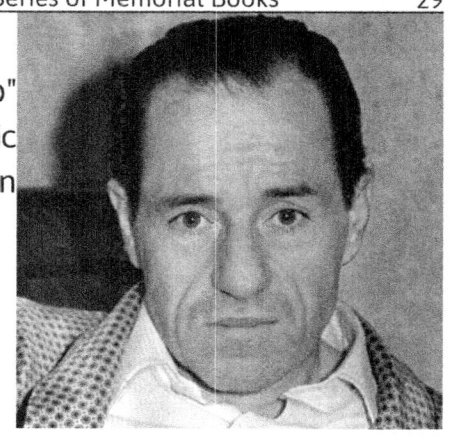

"Shadow Waltz" and "You're Getting to Be a Habit with Me" by Bing Crosby:

Bing Crosby's "Shadow Waltz" was a melodic delight that captured the imagination of music lovers during 1933. Another hit by Bing Crosby, "You're Getting to Be a Habit with Me" added to the charm of the year's musical landscape.

3.2 Renowned Musicians and Bands of '33

In 1933, the music scene was alive with the sounds of renowned musicians and bands who made their mark on the era. Here are some of the notable figures and groups that captured the hearts of music enthusiasts in '33:

1. Duke Ellington:

Duke Ellington, a prominent bandleader, composer, and pianist, continued to shape the world of jazz. His orchestra, the Duke Ellington Orchestra, was known for its innovative compositions and arrangements. In 1933, Ellington's "Sophisticated Lady" became a chart-topping hit, showcasing his musical genius.

2. Ethel Waters:

Ethel Waters, a remarkable jazz and blues vocalist, was celebrated for her soulful performances. Her rendition of "Stormy Weather" in 1933 left a lasting impact, making her one of the standout musical talents of the year.

3. Paul Whiteman:

Paul Whiteman, often referred to as the "King of Jazz" during the 1920s, continued to influence the music scene. His orchestra and collaborations with various musicians produced beloved tunes. In '33, his hit "Lover" resonated with audiences.

4. Irving Berlin:

Irving Berlin, a prolific composer and lyricist, contributed to the musical landscape of 1933 with his composition "Easter Parade." His songs were known for their catchy melodies and lyrical charm.

5. Bing Crosby:

Bing Crosby, a rising star in the world of popular music, began to establish his legacy. In '33, Crosby's rendition of "Shadow Waltz" and "You're Getting to Be a Habit with Me" showcased his distinctive crooning style.

6. Benny Goodman:

Benny Goodman, the "King of Swing," was a notable bandleader and clarinetist. Although he was on the cusp of his major breakthrough, he played a significant role in popularizing swing music, a genre that would dominate the music scene in the late '30s.

7. The Mills Brothers:

The Mills Brothers, a close-harmony vocal group, were known for their innovative use of vocal mimicry, creating the sound of musical instruments with their voices. Their hits like "Dinah" and "Lazy Bones" charmed audiences in 1933.

8. Louis Armstrong:

Louis Armstrong, a jazz legend and virtuoso trumpeter, continued to leave an indelible mark on the music world. His innovative solos and scat singing in songs like "I Cover the Waterfront" showcased his unparalleled talent.

Activity: Music Lyrics Challenge - Guess the Song Lyrics from '33

Test your knowledge of '33 music with this fun lyrics challenge! See if you can match the lyrics to the songs mentioned in the chapter.

Directions: Match the given song lyrics from 1933 to their respective songs. Can you correctly identify which song each set of lyrics belongs to?

Lyrics:
1. "Don't know why there's no sun up in the sky."
2. "But when you're walkin' down that street and you ain't had enough to eat."
3. "Oh, how I sigh for the touch of your lips, dear."
4. "I'll be all that I am, just your lover."
5. "In your Easter bonnet, with all the frills upon it."
6. "She's just a gold digger, say, why do you make her feel like a million?"

Songs:
   a. "Stormy Weather" by Ethel Waters
   b. "Sophisticated Lady" by Duke Ellington
   c. "Gold Digger's Song" by Dick Powell
   d. "Lover" by Paul Whiteman
   e. "Easter Parade" by Irving Berlin
   f. "The Last Round-Up" by Billy Hill
   g. "Shadow Waltz" and "You're Getting to Be a Habit with Me" by Bing Crosby

Chapter 4: Sports in 1933:
A Journey Through the World of Athletics

4.1 Athletic Achievements and Memorable Victories

In 1933, the world of sports was filled with extraordinary achievements, thrilling victories, and unforgettable moments. From chess to tennis, boxing to golf, cycling to football, this chapter explores the athletic feats that defined the year. Join us on a journey through a year when sports became a source of inspiration, creating legends and leaving an indelible mark on history.

Australian Championships Tennis:

Jan 30 Australian Championships Men's Tennis: Jack Crawford wins his 3rd straight Australian title; beats Keith Gledhill of the US 2-6, 7-5, 6-3, 6-2

Jan 30 Australian Championships Women's Tennis, Melbourne: Joan Hartigan Bathurst beats Coral McInnes Buttsworth 6-4, 6-3

Chess:

The world of chess saw the rise of Vera Menchik, an exceptional chess player whose remarkable skills and strategic thinking left a lasting impact on the game. Her contributions to the world of chess were widely recognized during this year.

French Men's Tennis Open:

Jun 5 In the realm of tennis, Australian Jack Crawford achieved a significant milestone by winning his first and only French Men's Tennis Open title. He defeated the home favorite, Henri Cochet, in an exciting match with a score of 8-6, 6-1, 6-3, showcasing his prowess on the clay courts of France.

Boxing Title Fight:

June 29 Italian boxer Primo Carnera delivered a knockout blow to the American defending champion Jack Sharkey. This victory, achieved at Madison Square Garden in New York City, earned Carnera the lineal world heavyweight title. His win made him the third European boxer to hold this prestigious title.

Wimbledon Men's Tennis:

Jul 7 The Wimbledon Men's Tennis Championship witnessed Australian Jack Crawford's triumph as he secured his only Wimbledon singles title. He faced fierce competition from American Ellsworth Vines, ultimately winning with a score of 4-6, 11-9, 6-2, 2-6, 6-4 in a thrilling match.

British Golf Open

Jul 8 In the world of golf, Denny Shute emerged as the victor in the British Open Men's Golf Championship. His impressive performance at St. Andrews allowed him to defeat fellow American Craig Wood by a margin of five strokes in a 36-hole playoff held on a Saturday, marking Shute's first and only Open title.

PGA Championship

Aug 13 The PGA Championship in Men's Golf took place at Blue Mound Country Club, where the legendary Gene Sarazen secured victory. Sarazen's triumph was marked by his impressive performance, defeating Willie Goggin with a score of 5 & 4, earning him his third PGA Championship title and his sixth major win.

IBU heavyweight title

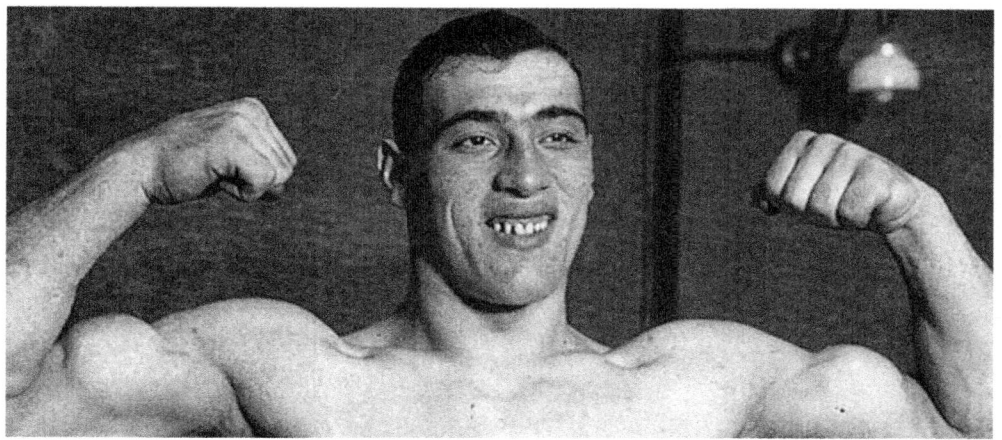

Oct 22 In the sport of boxing, Italian boxer Primo Carnera successfully defended his IBU heavyweight title. He faced Spanish challenger Paulino Uzcudun and secured victory on points in a memorable bout that took place in Rome, Italy.

CFL Grey Cup

Dec 9 In Canadian football, the CFL Grey Cup was a closely contested match held at Athletic Park in Sarnia. The Toronto Argonauts edged past the Sarnia Imperials with a score of 4-3, clinching their third championship title.

4.2 American Sports: Champions and Championship Moments

World Series:

Oct 7 In baseball, the New York Giants clinched the World Series by defeating the Washington Senators with a score of 4-3. The series concluded with the Giants winning four games to one. This victory was a significant moment in baseball history.

Stanley Cup:

In ice hockey, the Stanley Cup Finals took place at the Maple Leaf Gardens in Toronto, Ontario. The New York Rangers faced the Toronto Maple Leafs in an intense showdown, with the Rangers emerging victorious with a 1-0 overtime win. This marked the first best-of-four Finals series, highlighting the growing popularity of the sport.

National Football League:

Dec 17 The National Football League (NFL) Championship, the first title game of its kind, was held at Wrigley Field in Chicago. The Chicago Bears secured a thrilling victory by defeating the New York Giants with a score of 23-21. This game is notable for introducing the "Bronko Nagurski Rule," which made the forward pass legal from anywhere behind the line of scrimmage.

US Ladies' Figure Skating championship

Mar 18 The US Ladies' Figure Skating Championship was won by the talented Maribel Vinson, who showcased her remarkable skills and artistry on the ice. Her achievement in figure skating was celebrated during this championship.

US Golf Open:

Jun 10 US Open Men's Golf, North Shore CC: Amateur Johnny Goodman outlasts Ralph Guldahl by a single stroke to win his only major championship

Activity: Sports Trivia - Test Your Knowledge of 1933 Sports History

Let's dive into the exciting world of 1933 sports history. Put on your thinking cap and see how well you remember the memorable sports events and champions from this era.

1.Who was the renowned chess player whose exceptional skills left a lasting impact in 1933?
- a) Vera Menchik
- b) Mikhail Botvinnik
- c) José Capablanca
- d) Boris Spassky

2.Australian Jack Crawford achieved a significant milestone in tennis in 1933 by winning his first and only title at which major tennis event?
- a) Wimbledon
- b) US Open
- c) French Open
- d) Australian Open

3.In a memorable boxing match at Madison Square Garden, Italian boxer Primo Carnera knocked out American defending champion Jack Sharkey to become the lineal world heavyweight champion. When did this historic fight take place?
- a) May 21, 1933
- b) June 29, 1933
- c) July 4, 1933
- d) August 15, 1933

4.Who emerged as the Wimbledon Men's Tennis champion in 1933 after defeating American Ellsworth Vines in an intense match?
- a) Bjorn Borg
- b) Rafael Nadal
- c) Jack Crawford
- d) Rod Laver

5.Denny Shute secured a significant victory in golf in 1933 at which prestigious golf championship, defeating fellow American Craig Wood?
- a) US Open
- b) The Masters
- c) The Open Championship (British Open)
- d) PGA Championship

6.The PGA Championship in Men's Golf was won by the legendary Gene Sarazen in 1933. How many PGA Championship titles did this victory mark for him, and how many majors did he win in total?
- a) 2 PGA Championship titles, 5 majors
- b) 3 PGA Championship titles, 6 majors
- c) 4 PGA Championship titles, 7 majors
- d) 5 PGA Championship titles, 8 majors

7.In a thrilling boxing match in Rome, Italy, Italian boxer Primo Carnera faced a Spanish challenger to retain the IBU heavyweight title. Who was his challenger?
- a) Max Schmeling
- b) Jack Johnson
- c) Joe Louis
- d) Paulino Uzcudun

8.The Toronto Argonauts clinched their third championship in which Canadian sport, and where did this historic match take place?
- a) Stanley Cup
- b) Grey Cup
- c) The Memorial Cup
- d) Royal Winter Fair

Enjoy the multiple-choice quiz and see how well you remember the exciting sports history of 1933!

Chapter 5: Pop Culture, Fashion, and Popular Leisure Activities

5.1 Fashion Flashback: What the World Wore in '33

The year 1933 brought distinct fashion trends and styles that reflected the era's unique character. Both men and women embraced a sense of elegance and sophistication, while staying true to the spirit of the times.

Women's fashion:

1. Soft and feminine looks

Women's fashion in 1933 embraced a soft and feminine aesthetic. The silhouettes featured gentle curves, which were a departure from the boyish, straight styles of the previous decade.

2. Flowing full skirts

The full skirt was a prominent feature, often flowing gracefully around the wearer. These skirts brought an air of romance to women's fashion.

3. Bobs and finger waves

The bob haircut, characterized by its short length, was in vogue. Many women also sported finger waves, a wavy and sleek hairstyle that complemented the overall look.

4. Pump - Peep toe shoes

Women's shoes featured classic pumps and peep-toe styles. These elegant and often heeled shoes completed the sophisticated appearance.

5. Puffed or butterfly sleeves

Sleeves gained attention with puffed or butterfly shapes, adding an element of whimsy to dresses and blouses.

Men

1. Wide pointed lapels

Men's fashion in 1933 emphasized wide pointed lapels on suits and jackets, giving a strong and confident look.

2. Oxfords - Wingtip shoes

Footwear was characterized by classic Oxfords and wingtip shoes, offering both elegance and comfort to men's fashion.

3. High waisted pants

High-waisted trousers were popular among men, emphasizing the waist and adding an element of formality to their outfits.

4. V - neck sweaters

V-neck sweaters were a staple in men's wardrobes. These sweaters exuded a sense of smart casualness.

5. Fedora hats - Newsboy caps

Headwear was essential in 1933, with men often seen wearing fedora hats for a formal look or newsboy caps for a more relaxed style.

5.2. Entertainment and Hobbies

The early 1930s, including 1933, were marked by an array of entertainment and hobbies that provided a much-needed escape from the challenges of the era. These pastimes and diversions captured the imagination of people worldwide, offering moments of joy and respite.

1. Entertainment
Cinema:

The 1930s marked the golden age of Hollywood cinema. Iconic films like "King Kong," "Little Women," and "Duck Soup" graced the silver screen in 1933, captivating audiences with their cinematic magic.

Music:

The world of music was rich and diverse. Chart-topping hits like "Stormy Weather" by Ethel Waters and "Sophisticated Lady" by Duke Ellington set the musical backdrop for the year, reflecting the era's emotions and sentiments.

Radio:

Radio continued to be a prominent source of entertainment, with radio dramas, comedy shows, and music broadcasts providing a connection to the wider world. Families gathered around the radio for evening entertainment.

Literature:

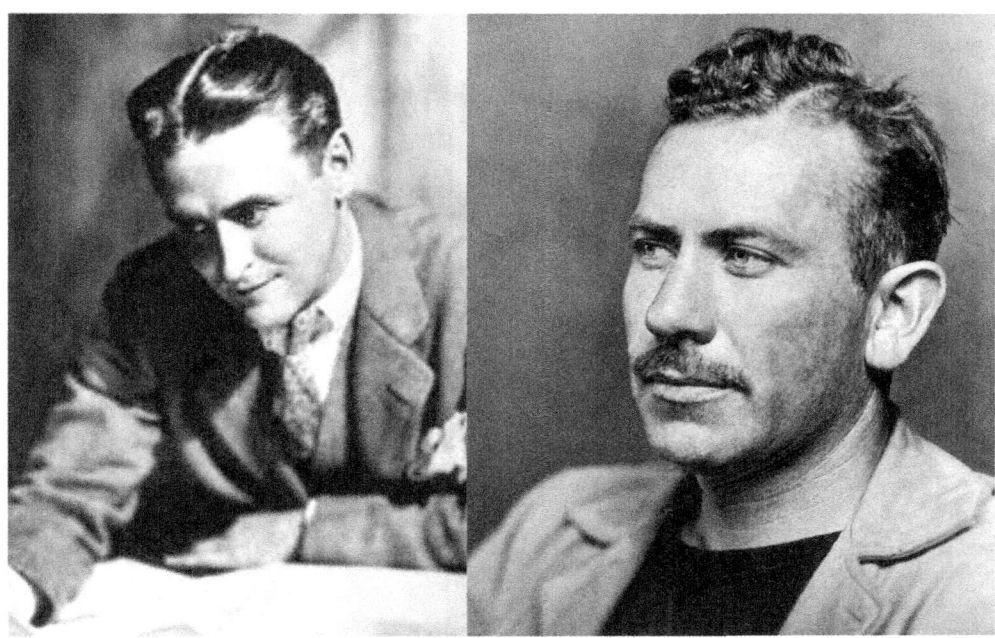

Books, magazines, and newspapers remained a cherished source of entertainment and information. Writers like F. Scott Fitzgerald and John Steinbeck produced notable works during the period, contributing to the literary landscape.

2. Hobbies
Dance:

Dancing was a beloved hobby in the 1930s, with dance styles like the foxtrot, Charleston, and swing gaining popularity. Dance halls and clubs were vibrant social spaces.

Board Games:

Board games provided indoor entertainment for families and friends. Classics like Monopoly and Scrabble were introduced during this period, becoming enduring favorites.

Collecting:

Collecting hobbies thrived, from stamp and coin collecting to the fascination with "dime store" novelties and collectible cards. These hobbies added an element of discovery to leisure time.

Photography:

Photography became an increasingly popular hobby as cameras became more accessible. People captured their lives and moments in time, contributing to the preservation of history.

5.3 Slang of '33 - The language of the Era
The 1930s had a language of its own, filled with colorful slang that reflected the spirit of the time. In 1933, people used these vibrant expressions to communicate and connect, infusing their conversations with a unique flair.

Clam bake ~ Fun time

"Let's have a clam bake!" This slang term was an invitation to have a rollicking and enjoyable time. Just as a clam bake was a social gathering where people had fun and relished seafood, using this phrase meant it was time for a good, lighthearted get-together.

Slip me a five ~ Shake hands

"Slip me a five, buddy." This phrase had nothing to do with money but was actually an invitation to shake hands or offer a friendly greeting. It was a way of engaging with someone in a cordial and amicable manner.

Giggle Juice ~ Alcohol

"Care for some giggle juice?" This playful term referred to alcohol, particularly alcoholic beverages that could bring about laughter or merriment. During the Prohibition era, when alcohol was banned, people often used inventive language to talk about it.

Blow Your Wig ~ Excited

"That news will blow your wig!" If something was going to "blow your wig," it meant that the news or information was so thrilling or astonishing that it might figuratively blow your hat or wig off your head. It was a way of expressing excitement.

Grifter ~ Con man

"Watch out for that grifter." A "grifter" referred to a con man or swindler who aimed to deceive and cheat people, often through scams or fraudulent schemes. Being aware of grifters was essential to avoid falling victim to their tricks.

Activity:
Fashion Design Coloring Page - Create Your '33-Inspired Outfit

Share your 1933 photos,
Don't forget to show off your fabulous '33 fashion

Chapter 6: Technological Advancements and Popular Cars

6.1 Innovations That Shaped the Future

The year 1933 was marked by several groundbreaking technological advancements that laid the foundation for future developments. These innovations not only contributed to scientific progress but also shaped the way people lived and enjoyed their leisure time.

Electron Microscope - Germany by Ernst Ruska:

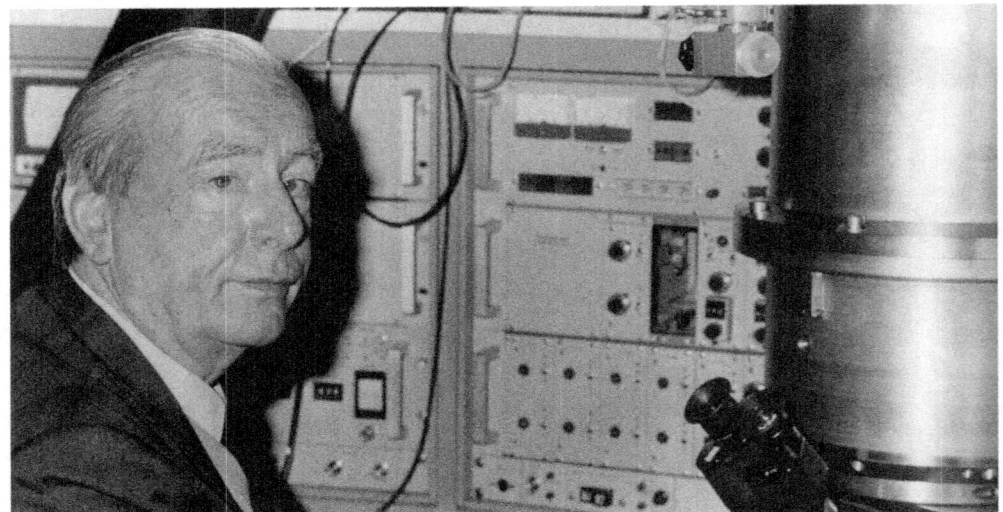

In 1933, German scientist Ernst Ruska made significant strides in electron microscopy. The electron microscope was a revolutionary invention that allowed researchers to examine objects at an unprecedented level of detail. By using a beam of electrons to illuminate the object, the electron microscope surpassed the limitations of traditional light microscopes, enabling scientists to view structures at the nanoscale. This innovation had a profound impact on various scientific fields, including biology, materials science, and nanotechnology.

Drive-in Movie Theater - USA by Richard Hollingshead:

The concept of the drive-in movie theater was born in 1933, thanks to the vision of Richard Hollingshead in the United States. This novel approach to watching films allowed people to enjoy movies from the comfort of their own cars. The idea was simple: a large outdoor screen, a speaker system, and the convenience of staying in your car while watching a film. Drive-in theaters quickly gained popularity and became a symbol of American entertainment culture. They provided families and friends with a unique way to enjoy movies under the stars, making it a cherished pastime for generations.

Nuclear Reaction - Physicist Leo Szilard:

In 1933, physicist Leo Szilard had a groundbreaking idea that would alter the course of history. He conceived the concept of a nuclear chain reaction, which laid the theoretical foundation for the development of nuclear reactors and, eventually, the atomic bomb. This idea had profound implications, leading to scientific research into harnessing nuclear energy for both peaceful and destructive purposes. It eventually played a pivotal role in the development of nuclear power plants and the atomic age.

Machine Gun - Demonstrated by Japanese Scientist:

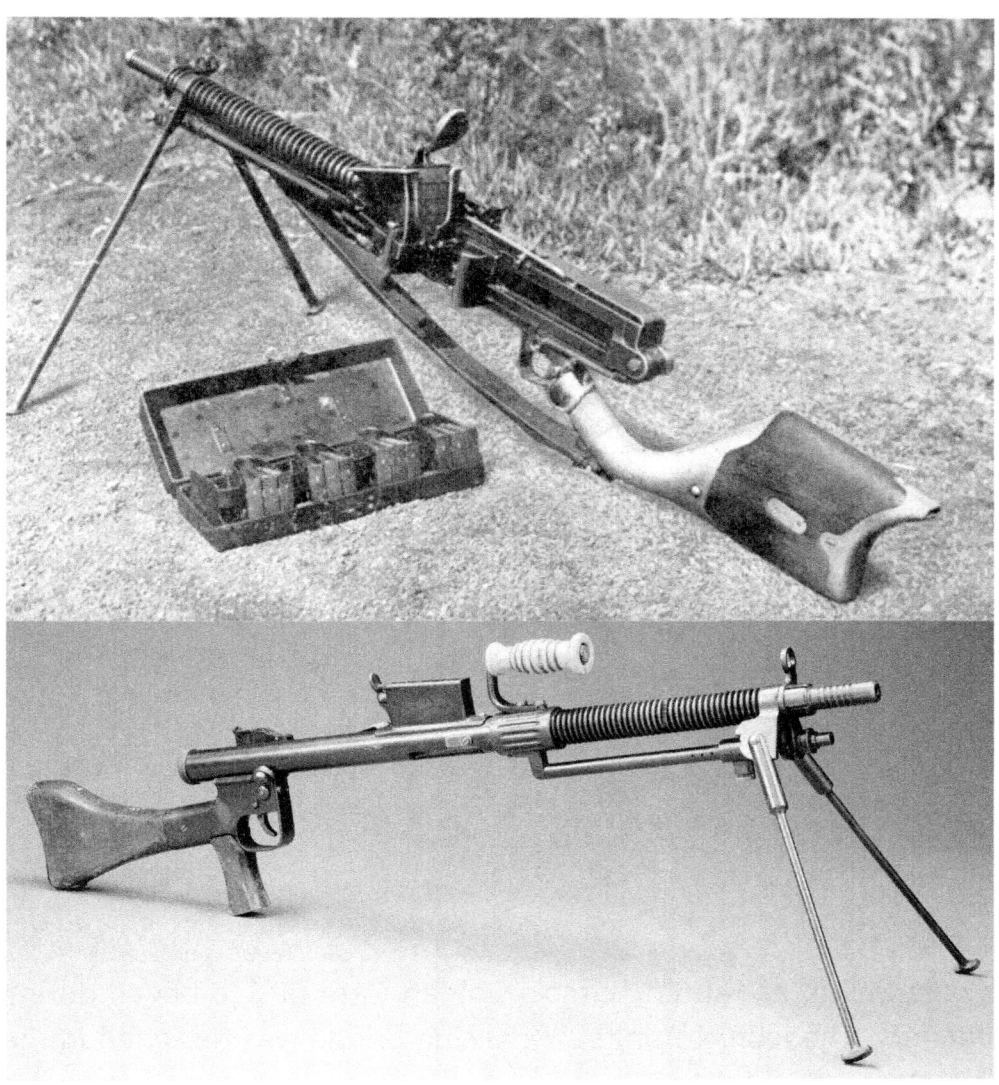

1933 saw a significant demonstration in the field of weaponry when a Japanese scientist showcased a machine gun capable of firing 1,000 rounds per minute. This innovation represented a major advancement in firearms technology, increasing the rate of fire and potentially revolutionizing military tactics. Machine guns would go on to play a crucial role in various conflicts, shaping the nature of warfare in the years to come.

Golden Gate Bridge Construction

Construction of San Francisco's Golden Gate Bridge began during January. The iconic orange suspension bridge was designed in the art deco style by Irving Morrow and the chief engineers were Joseph Strauss and Charles Ellis. It was completed in 1937 and connected the city of San Francisco and Marin County, California. The bridge spans 4,200 feet and is one of the longest and tallest suspension bridges in the world. It cost between $27 million and $35 million to build at the time and was financed by a bond measure due to a lack of readily available funds during the Great Depression.

6.2 The Automobiles of '33

The 1930s marked a significant era in the evolution of the automobile industry. In 1933, various car manufacturers introduced models that reflected the changing tastes and needs of consumers. These cars combined engineering innovations with stylistic changes that set them apart. Here are some of the notable automobiles of 1933:

Chevrolet Master:

The Chevrolet Master was part of the Chevrolet series for 1933, offering consumers a more powerful and spacious option. It featured a six-cylinder engine that provided improved performance and driving comfort. This model contributed to Chevrolet's reputation for delivering reliable and affordable vehicles.

Ford Model Y:

Ford introduced the Model Y in 1932, and it continued to be a popular choice in 1933. This compact car was designed to be affordable and practical. Its small size and fuel efficiency made it suitable for the urban environment, and it became a staple of British roads.

Plymouth PC:

The Plymouth PC, launched in 1933, was Plymouth's response to the economic challenges of the Great Depression. It was positioned as a budget-friendly alternative in the Plymouth lineup, offering consumers an affordable option while retaining the quality and durability associated with the brand.

Buick Series 50:

Buick's Series 50, also known as the Buick Special, was a well-regarded model in 1933. It was praised for its combination of style and performance. The Series 50 featured a straight-eight engine, providing a smooth and powerful driving experience.

Packard Twelve:

For those seeking luxury and performance, the Packard Twelve was a standout choice. Known for its V12 engine and elegant design, this car catered to an upscale clientele. It was a symbol of prestige and quality, demonstrating Packard's commitment to craftsmanship.

Chrysler Imperial:

The Chrysler Imperial was a flagship model for Chrysler in 1933, offering a blend of elegance and engineering. It was powered by a straight-eight engine and featured luxurious amenities. This car exemplified the luxury segment of the market.

Activity: Cars 1933 - Wordsearch

Introduction: Find the names of popular car models from 1933 in the puzzle below

```
U C Q U A L T O R W F L W K V P
I H O J M U N W C H G R O O U A
S E H R N A U Y E F Q H W R Y C
R V J O D B F X S L K G E M F K
I R Z P C M U G H M R B H Z M A
A O E X P J O I N D B U D G B R
Q L R P H S M D C W L I R T W D
W E X C L T Q K E K B C C U X T
Y T K M U B C X G L S K J F J W
Q M Z R Q G E Y L S Y E U J Q E
O A N Z F Q Y S D T P J R Y X L
A S T O N R S G V J Q P P I D V
P T Y M O U T H P C R X I T E E
O E G S O E N N V A Z C Z O R S
G R K C A W B J P J D Z M U F F
C H R Y S L E R I M P E R I A L
```

Chrysler Imperial
Packard Twelve
Buick Series 50

Plymouth PC
Ford Model Y
Chevrolet Master
Buick

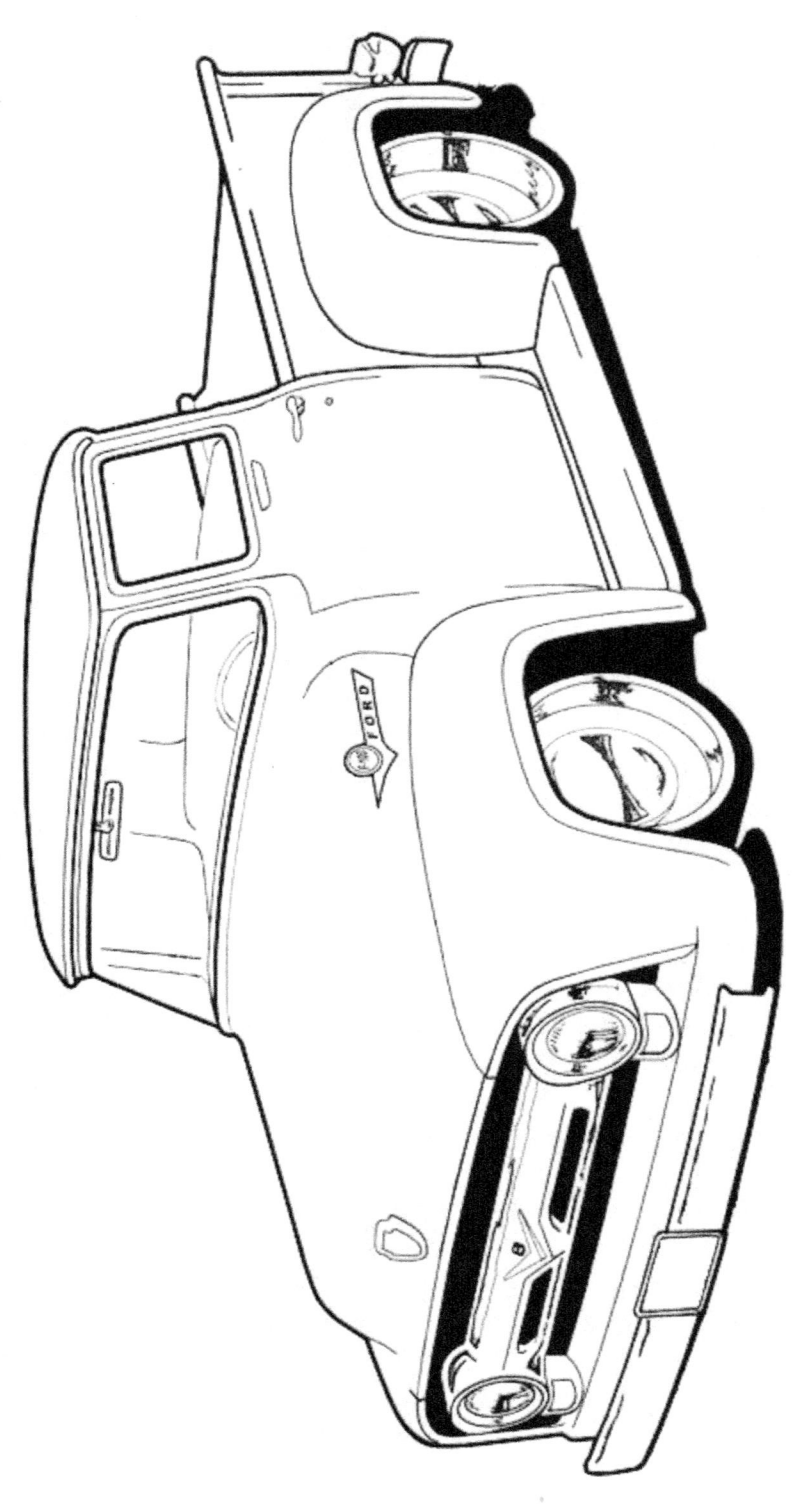

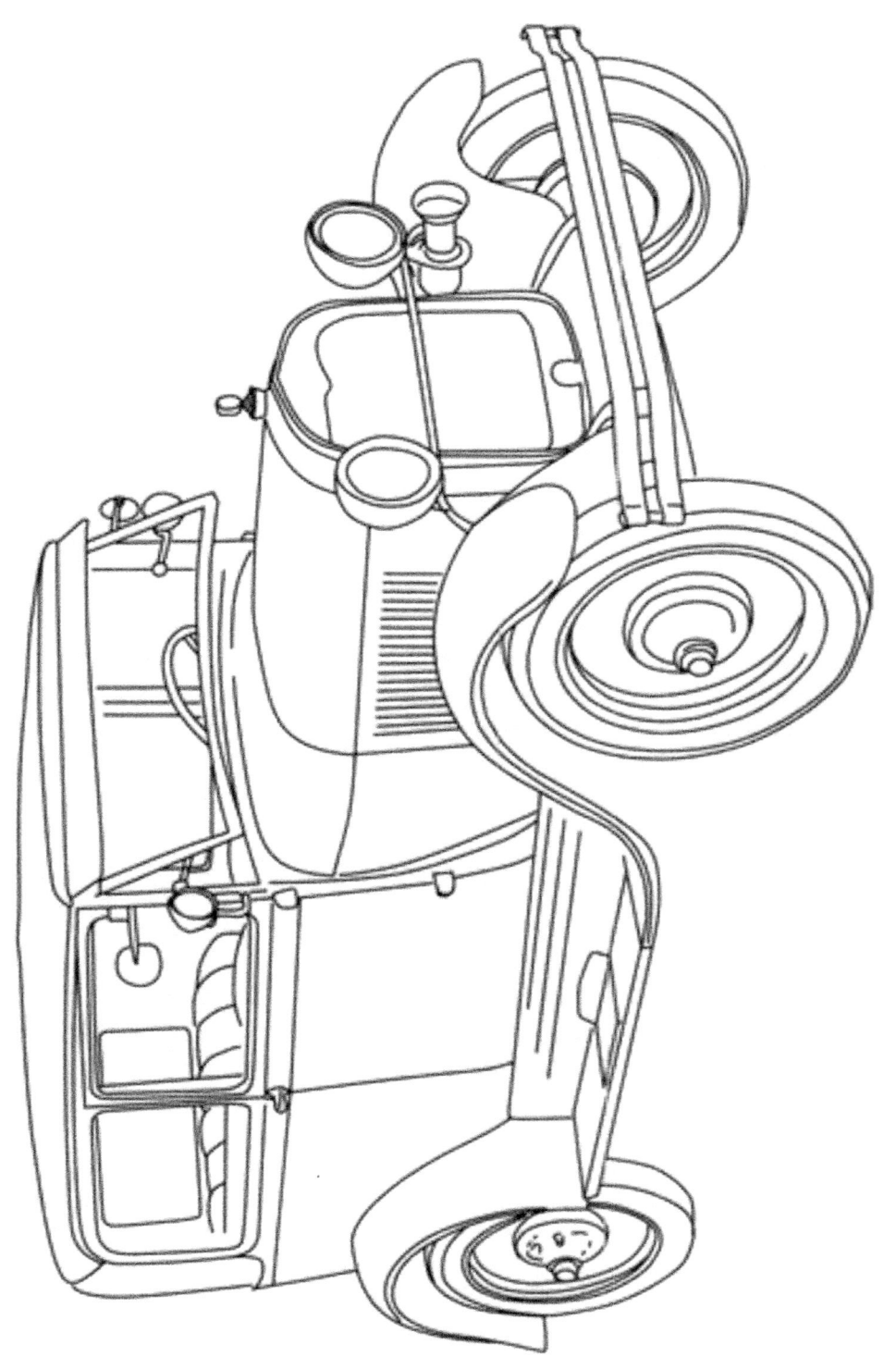

Chapter 7:
Stats and the Cost of Things

7.1 The Price Tag: Cost of Living in 1933

The year 1933 was marked by significant economic challenges, primarily due to the Great Depression. As a result, the cost of living during this period was notably affected. Here are some key aspects of the cost of living in 1933:

- New house $5,570.00

- Average Monthly Rent $18.00 per month
- Average wages per year $1,550.00
- A loaf of bread $0.07
- A gallon of gas $0.10
- A movie ticket $0.23
- A first class stamp $0.03

- A LB of Hamburger Meat 11 cents

- Vacuum Cleaner $17.75

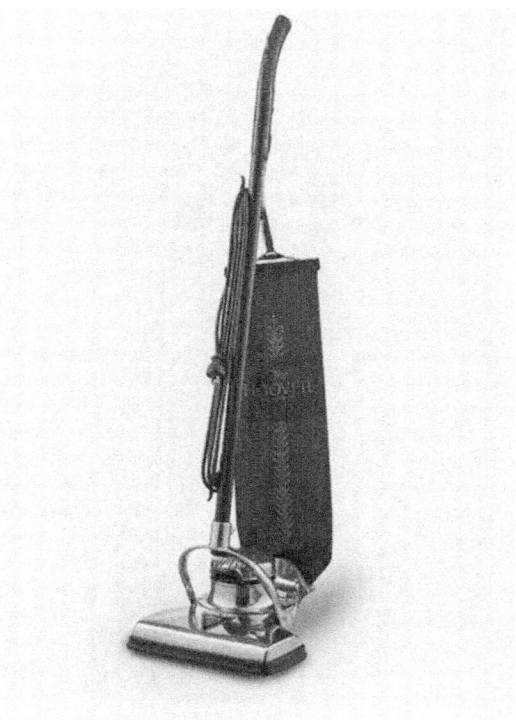

- Plymouth 6 Car $445.00

- 1933 Radio $52.00

- Newport Boulevard Ladies Hat $1.69

- Silk and Rayon Stockings 39 cents a Pair
- Health Building Tonic 89 cents
- Campbells Vegetable Soup 11 cents
- Dozen eggs $0.20
- A gallon of milk $0.25

Activity:
1933 Shopping List Challenge

Let's take a step back in time to the year 1933 and imagine you're heading to the store with a shopping list. Your task is to create a shopping list for essential items you'd need for your household during this year, keeping in mind the cost of living and the economic conditions of the Great Depression. Here's how the challenge works:

Instructions:

- Shopping List: Create a shopping list for essential items you'd need for your household in 1933. You can include items such as groceries, household supplies, clothing, or anything else you think was necessary during that time.
- Item Descriptions: Next to each item on your shopping list, provide a brief description of the item and its estimated 1933 price. You can use the information from Chapter 7: "Stats and the Cost of Things."
- Total Cost: Calculate the total cost of your shopping list based on the 1933 prices you've provided.
- Share Your List: Once you've completed your shopping list, descriptions, and total cost, share it with friends or family and discuss the differences between shopping in 1933 and today.

Sample Shopping List:

- Bread - A loaf of bread (7 cents)
- Eggs - A dozen eggs (20 cents)
- Rent - Monthly apartment rent ($18)
- Gasoline - A gallon of gasoline (10 cents)

- Car - New car (e.g., Ford Model Y, $600)
- Shirt - Men's dress shirt ($2)
- Dress - Women's dress ($3.50)
- Shoes - A pair of shoes (e.g., Oxfords, $4.75)
- Toothpaste - A tube of toothpaste (15 cents)

Total Cost: $79.74

Feel free to adjust your shopping list based on your household's needs and preferences. This activity provides a glimpse into the economic conditions and costs of living during 1933, allowing you to compare them to the present day.

SHOPPING List

	Item	Price	# Units	Total Price
☐				
☐				
☐				
☐				
☐				
☐				
☐				
☐				
☐				
☐				
☐				
☐				
☐				
☐				
☐				
☐				
☐				
☐				
☐				
☐				
☐				
☐				
			Total	

Chapter 8:
The Famous Wedding of 1933

Love was in the air in 1933, and several famous couples tied the knot, capturing the attention and admiration of the public and the media. Here are some of the notable weddings that took place during the year:

1. Charlie Chaplin and Paulette Goddard (June 1)

Renowned actor and filmmaker Charlie Chaplin, aged 44, exchanged vows with the talented actress Paulette Goddard, who was 22 at the time. Their union was a significant moment in the world of entertainment, blending Chaplin's cinematic genius with Goddard's acting prowess.

2. John Wayne and Josephine Saenz (June 24)

On June 24, iconic American actor John Wayne, at the age of 26, married Josephine Saenz, who was 25, in a ceremony held in Los Angeles, California. Their wedding marked the beginning of a personal journey together, celebrated by fans and well-wishers.

3. Fred Astaire and Phyllis Livingston Potter (July 12)

Fred Astaire, often recognized as one of the greatest male stars of all time, wed American socialite Phyllis Livingston Potter on July 12. Their union brought together the world of dance and high society, making it a memorable event in the world of entertainment.

4. Jack Dempsey and Hannah Williams (July 18)

American heavyweight boxing champion Jack Dempsey, aged 38, married American Broadway singer and actress Hannah Williams, who was 22, on July 18. Their wedding combined the worlds of sports and entertainment, drawing the attention of fans and admirers.

5. Hedy Lamarr and Friedrich Mandl (August 10)

Austro-Hungarian actress Hedy Kreissler, later known as Hedy Lamarr, was only 18 when she married Austrian arms manufacturer Hirtenberger Patronen-Fabrik chairman Friedrich Mandl, aged 33, on August 10. Their wedding brought together glamour and industry, and Hedy Lamarr would go on to become an iconic figure in both the entertainment and scientific worlds.

6. Victor Fleming and Lucile Rosson (September 26)

On September 26, director Victor Fleming, aged 44, exchanged vows with Lucile Rosson. Their wedding marked a personal milestone for the man behind the camera, celebrated by those in the film industry.

7. Johnny Weissmuller and Lupe Vélez (October 8)

Renowned American actor Johnny Weissmuller, famous for his portrayal of Tarzan, married Mexican actress Lupe Vélez on October 8. Their union combined the worlds of Hollywood and international cinema.

8. Gary Cooper and Veronica Balfe (December 15)

American actor Gary Cooper, at the age of 32, wed American actress Veronica Balfe, who was 20 at the time. Their wedding took place at her mother's home on Park Avenue in New York City, becoming a notable event in the world of film and celebrity.

Activity:
Famous Wedding Trivia 1933 Edition

1. Who was the renowned actor and filmmaker who married the talented actress Paulette Goddard on June 1, 1933?
a) Charlie Chaplin
b) John Wayne
c) Fred Astaire
d) Gary Cooper

2. On June 24, 1933, which iconic American actor tied the knot with Josephine Saenz in Los Angeles, California?
a) Charlie Chaplin
b) John Wayne
c) Fred Astaire
d) Jack Dempsey

3. Fred Astaire, often considered one of the greatest male stars of all time, married American socialite Phyllis Livingston Potter on July 12, 1933. What was the specialty of Fred Astaire?
a) Singing
b) Dancing
c) Directing
d) Comedy

4. American heavyweight boxing champion Jack Dempsey married American Broadway singer and actress Hannah Williams on July 18, 1933. What was Jack Dempsey's profession?
a) Actor
b) Musician
c) Politician
d) Boxer

5.On August 10, 1933, an Austro-Hungarian actress named Hedy Kreissler married Austrian arms manufacturer Friedrich Mandl. What name is Hedy Kreissler more famously known as?
a) Hedy Lamarr
b) Audrey Hepburn
c) Katharine Hepburn
d) Ingrid Bergman

6.Director Victor Fleming exchanged vows with Lucile Rosson on September 26, 1933. What is Victor Fleming's claim to fame in the world of entertainment?
a) Pioneering special effects
b) Iconic film director
c) Renowned actor
d) Leading screenwriter

7.On October 8, 1933, renowned American actor Johnny Weissmuller, famous for his portrayal of Tarzan, married which Mexican actress?
a) Maria Felix
b) Dolores del Rio
c) Lupe Vélez
d) Katy Jurado

8.The wedding of American actor Gary Cooper and American actress Veronica Balfe took place on December 15, 1933, at her mother's home on Park Avenue in New York City. How old was Gary Cooper at the time of their wedding?
a) 25
b) 30
c) 32
d) 40

Unleash your creativity and bring the famous 1933 wedding to life with vibrant colors in this exciting coloring wedding picture activity

We have heartfelt thank-you gifts for you

As a token of our appreciation for joining us on this historical journey through 1933, we've included a set of cards and stamps inspired by the year of 1933. These cards are your canvas to capture the essence of the past. We encourage you to use them as inspiration for creating your own unique cards, sharing your perspective on the historical moments we've explored in this book. Whether it's a holiday greeting or a simple hello to a loved one, these cards are your way to connect with the history we've uncovered together.

Happy creating!

Activity Answers

Chapter 1:

ACROSS:
2. Dust Bowl
5. Makoto Saito
6. Franklin D. Roosevelt
7. Adolf Hitler

DOWN:
1. Joseph Stalin
3. Loch Ness Monster
4. Ramsay MacDonald

Chapter 2:
1. C
2. A
3. A
4. C
5. C
6. D
7. C
8. B
9. C
10. C

Chapter 3:
1. a
2. f
3. d
4. g
5. e
6. c

Chapter 4:
1. A
2. C
3. B
4. C
5. C
6. B
7. D
8. B

Chapter 8:
1. A)Charlie Chaplin.
2. B)John Wayne.
3. B)Dancing
4. D)Boxer
5. A)Hedy Lamarr
6. B)Iconic film director
7. C)Lupe Vélez
8. D)32

Chapter 6:

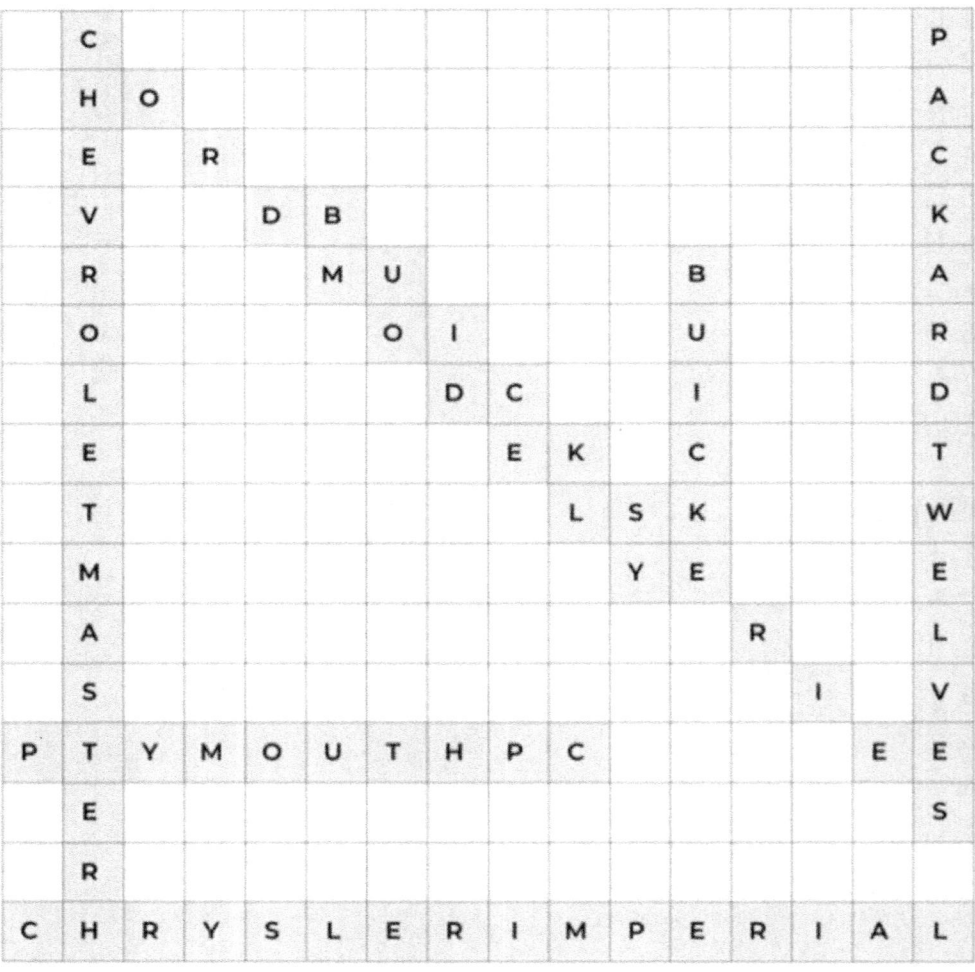

Embracing 1933: A Grateful Farewell

Embracing 1933: A Grateful Farewell
Thank you for joining us on this journey through a year that holds a special place in our hearts. Whether you experienced 1933 firsthand or through the pages of this book, we hope it brought you moments of joy, nostalgia, and connection to a time that will forever shine brightly in our memories.

Share Your Thoughts and Help Us Preserve History

Your support and enthusiasm for this journey mean the world to us. We invite you to share your thoughts, leave a review, and keep the spirit of '33 alive. As we conclude our adventure, we look forward to more journeys through the annals of history together. Until then, farewell and thank you for the memories.

We would like to invite you to explore more of our fantastic world by scanning the QR code below. There you can easily get free ebooks from us and receive so many surprises.

Copyright © Edward Art Lab 2023

All rights reserved. No part of this publication may be reproduced, distributed, or transmitted in any form or by any means, including photocopying, recording, or other electronic or mechanical methods, without the prior written permission of the publisher, except in the case of brief quotations embodied in critical reviews and certain other noncommercial uses permitted by copyright law.

NOTE

NOTE

NOTE

TO DO LIST

- ○ ------------------------------
- ○ ------------------------------
- ○ ------------------------------
- ○ ------------------------------
- ○ ------------------------------
- ○ ------------------------------
- ○ ------------------------------
- ○ ------------------------------
- ○ ------------------------------
- ○ ------------------------------
- ○ ------------------------------
- ○ ------------------------------
- ○ ------------------------------

well done!

TO DO LIST

- _____
- _____
- _____
- _____
- _____
- _____
- _____
- _____
- _____
- _____
- _____
- _____
- _____
- _____

well done!

To Do List

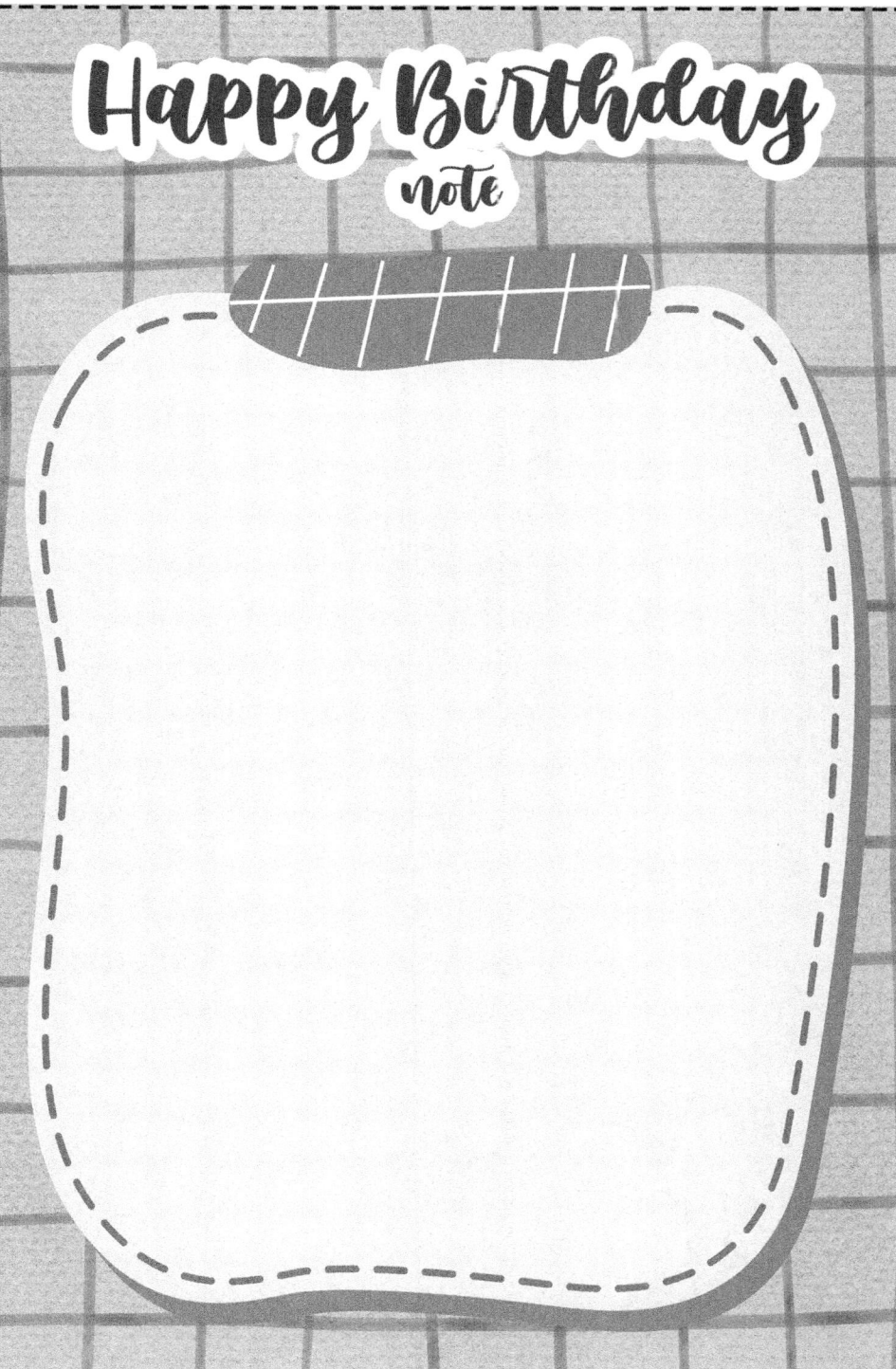

Happy Birthday
note

Happy Birthday
note

TO DO LIST

Name: _____ Day: _____ Month: _____

No	To Do List	Yes	No

TO DO LIST

Name: _____   Day: _____   Month: _____

No	To Do List	Yes	No

NOTE

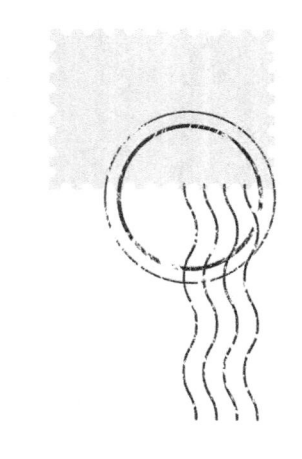

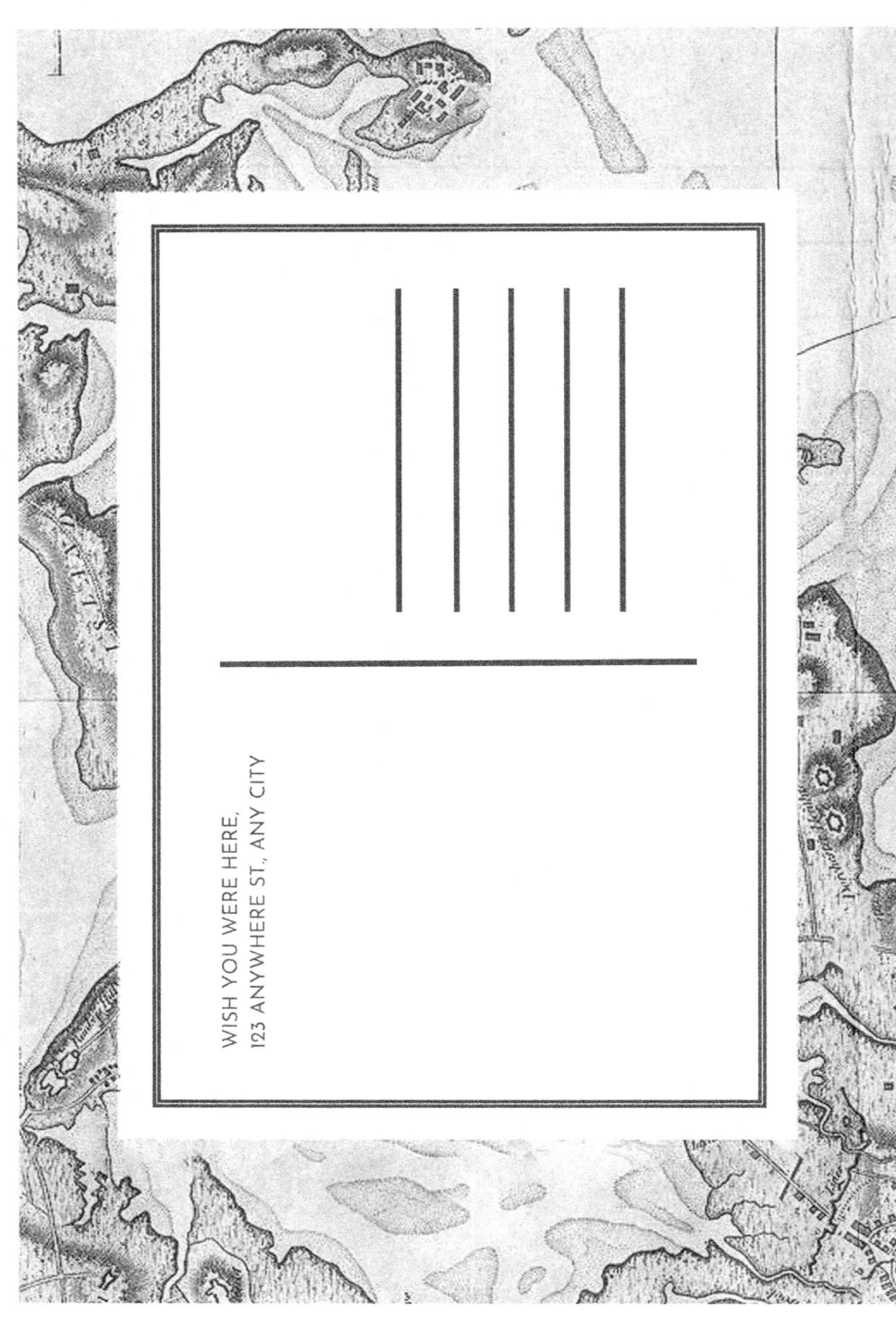

HAPPY BIRTHDAY NOTE

TO DO LIST

Name: _____   Day: _____   Month: _____

No	To Do List	Yes	No

Remember This!

Printed in Great Britain
by Amazon